PEARLS
OF
WISDOM

PEARLS
OF
WISDOM

BY
NINA
KELLY

Empress Publishing
Coquitlam, British Columbia, Canada

First Edition
Second Printing, 1991

Jacket and cover designed by Nina Kelly.

Published by
Empress Publishing
738 Austin Avenue
Coquitlam, British Columbia V3K 3N1
Canada

Canadian Cataloguing In Publication Data

Kelly, Nina
          Pearls of Wisdom

Poems
ISBN 1-55056-057-3

          I. Title
PR6061.E49P43 1990   821'.914   C90-090427-5

Manufactured in Canada

*This book is dedicated to my
two lovely daughters,
Antoinette and Nina*

Acknowledgements

This page is dedicated to those who have supported and encouraged my muse. Roger Foderingham, who bought me my first poetry book. Jane Pinnell, who first encouraged me to recite my verse. My heartiest appreciation to Delores Attios, Mary Marzano, the Pinawor gang, Eileen and Chris Johnston, and my Irish family, too numerous to mention individually. There are many others that space does not permit on this page, but for whom there is always room in my heart for the memory of their encouragement.

TABLE OF CONTENTS

TABLE OF CONTENTS

WINNING

Give a big smile
It's been there all the while
And start today to live the way
You should have lived before
Take courage to change the future
To a joy that you'll adore

You'll just have to begin
It will come from within
Clear out your clutter
It's mind over matter

You won't stumble or fall
There will be no great wall
You don't need my hand
Take your stand

And give a big smile
It's been there all the while

Ach, that's not a smile, that's only a grin
Try again, you know you can win!

A FRIEND AT THE END

Who are you? My dear friend?
I thought I knew you or is this a trend?
I recall you telling me you'll go far
Or is life for you a deep, wide scar

Tell me about your now and then
Is it so painful you can't say when?
Can't you tell I am your friend
And will always be until the end.

I'll give you the courage to get up and go
But your destination you must know.
I'll instill in you how to create
You'll soon learn how to participate

And when you find your occupation,
That will be your destination.
You'll know who you are, my dear,
Anticipation will have no fear

A rotten day you need not spend
If you give up this ugly trend
You'll be surprised what you can do
With that former self that's really you

It'll be time well spent and satisfied
Restoring my friend who nearly died

KNOW WHAT TO EXPECT

To ponder great moments,
   and treasure all tokens
To gather around
   a beautiful crowd
Especially those
   of whom you are proud
That way your heart
   will never be broken
And people will listen
   when your words are spoken

Make plans that will pay
To serve you each day
Wake up and say
"I'm well on my way,
What a wonderful day!"

We have tests all the time
And that's where we shine
It's an option we have
and the courage we grab

By treasuring your pride,
Throw all boasts aside
Keep life a new bride
You have nothing to hide

There's no mastery to this
And it's heavenly bliss
To ponder great moments
   and treasure all tokens

A HERO

Feeling so strong of birthright
Born into a world so great
He was eager, strong and bright
Not knowing in life his fate

He had little comfort, but yet he prayed
As he laid on the ground, with his last grenade
He looks at the pictures of his Mum and Dad
Yes, in his short life that's all that he had

He felt like a great wanderer, yet nowhere to go
He dreamed he had travelled to places you'd know
His nickname was Dreamer, they all called him that
And his dreams were vivid, now as he sat

From over the seas, the rainbows were gleaming
Bringing with them a sun that was beaming
While in his ears, the bells were ringing
And in his eyes the tears were stinging

He never imagined lying in a derelict sight
For his purpose in life was to reach a great height
He still hopes to get there, but he doesn't know when
His heart is still in it, you can tell by his grin

To freedom he goes without his fears
Loud and clear, a message he hears
He ignores its warning powers
He begins to count the waning hours

A young Lad alone in the trenches
Still steadily counting his riches
He was born into a world so great
And a hero in life demands his own fate

THE PRICE I PAID

Spring is a super time,
    but summer is the best
Somehow lying in the sun,
    I've put my fears to rest
I think of all the blooms there are,
    and of their glorious color
Yet nothing takes the place today
    of my adorable lover

I wish that you were here with me,
    and not so far away
But there's a price for being a lover
    and that's the price I pay
Walking on the beach today
There were a thousand things to see
    and many words to say

I couldn't share a single thought,
    or even say your name
I can never speak a word of you,
    I'd surely die of shame
My thoughts were to follow you
    to the ends of the earth,
But that was well before
    I found you to be a flirt

Spring is a super time,
  but summer is the best
Somehow lying in the sun,
  I've put my worries to rest
I had a very sleepless night
And woke up with a fright
My thoughts were jumbled and confused
  but soon were put to right

I never wanted to tempt fate
My mind was always full of hate
For my lover's lifelong, loving mate
To tell the truth, I finally feel just great

I saw my life just flitter away,
  before my very eyes
I decided to put it in order,
  and get rid of this disguise
Somehow I found my long lost self,
  and I gathered up my pride
Oh, what a glorious feeling,
  never more to hide

ALL OR NOTHING

Seldom asking what's the price
All we say is, that's real nice
Nobody wants a piece or a slice
Offered this, we look twice

It is somewhat a ghastly shame
Yet, we have no single one to blame
There'd be nothing wrong if we turned to fame
No! To us it's just a game

The simple things are lost forever
Like sincerely talking about the weather
And the family really getting together
Inquiring the health of Auntie Heather

Instead we speak of the mighty dollar
That turns a whisper into a holler
We used to have a prodigy
Lately, it's just you and me

Often when we have something to say
We open our wallets and readily pay
We go to a counsellor, instead of a fight
Do you think that's quite right?

We don't have honesty, we only fake
In daily life we're on the make
Do we have a hobby anymore?
Think, are we really sure?

Nowadays we share the kids
Teaching them to tell great fibs
What happened to living with what we got
My! If we could, we'd have the lot

Can we say that we are really free?
He or she?
Or you and me?

KIDS

Kids change day by day
While we just stay the same old way
Most are helpful and kind
Please keep this in mind

When they are nice and swanky
We sometimes get very cranky
But aren't they really great
When they become our mate
We know that they are doing their part
When we see them help right from their heart

They become our pride and joy, like great apple pie
When we're on an all high
And I'll tell you why

We can appreciate their get up and go
Even though we're getting slow
Remembering we were like them in our youth
Sometimes dishonest and often uncouth
It could be jealousy, if we'd admit the truth

Are they lucky? Maybe not
Depending on life and what is their lot
Would you change, if you could?
Be honest, you know you would!

LIFE

Life is full of many risks
Some think it a game and play deplorable tricks
They forget that we can mold it as we wish
But can't turn a species such as fowl into fish

The thing in life to remember
And never to render
Is use what we have, make it the best
Often that turns out to be the right crest

You can wear a crown of precious jewels,
    silver and of gold
Often it requires of you
    that you be a little bold
There might be some who preach to us
    that we will never find
And tell us that we are so very much behind
But those are greatly insecure
While we are very, very sure
They should learn from us and heed
Even if they can not read

IF WE STAY TOGETHER

Pick out the memories, only the good
Bury the rest, you know you should.
Try to follow the love in your heart
If that doesn't work, you know you must part

If he loves another, just let him go
There's always someone for you, you know
For a cheater there is no magical cure
He could do it again, you can never be sure

Your life you fear that he will rule
If you let him, you're the fool
If you can't live without him 'cause he's the one you adore
If that be the case and you're really sure

If you're really in love and want to stay together,
Through thick and thin, in spite of the shredder
You'll have to banish bad thoughts day by day
There's no guarantee it will always pay

All through life there must be trust
Don't take it lightly, it's an absolute must
The affair can't be mentioned ever again
If you can do that, then you both can win

LOVE

You have instilled in me the greatest of passion
Before I met you it was only a ration
As you lie in bed next to me
An angel on earth is what I see.

HEAR WHAT I SAY

Gazing out the window, there's much to see
flavoring one's life with sights that are free
The birds fly high, often in a cluster
I want to fly high but my life's in a fluster

From my perch I gazed around
My eyes landed and I found the ground
The grass is all burnt from a frost so severe
Not looking green, it sure looks queer
It looks really dead and gone forever
That's not so... it's only the weather

It's remarkable how it all bounces back
Especially since it has had such an attack
It's often covered up for months at a time
When it is cleared it looks like twine
A change in the climate and you will see
Soon it will be as green as can be

I am telling myself that I mustn't fret
I have decided my life is not over yet
Just like the grass I'll bounce right back
Didn't I just have another attack?

I closed my eyes, I thought to think
My eyes opened wide, it was only a wink

I could see there was a bit of a breeze
Suddenly I was examining all of the trees
They are not all strong, straight or tall
Many are big yet many are small
Their limbs were all limp, they had drooped their head
There were even some that looked as if they were dead

They haven't given up, and I know why
One day they believe they'll see the sky
Like all things in life, they have to rely on another
To let in the light when they clear out the clutter

I have made peace with myself and I am willing to go
But until then I'm stealing the show.
I've opened my mind, I've let in the light
The sad thing is I'm suffering from fright.
I am seeing things now like never before
That often were there but behind a closed door.
People think of blindness as not seeing at all
And of stumbling around, often to fall.

I have lived a life that I thought was great
There was one thing wrong, I didn't have faith
I am certainly not going to be in a rut,
I'm opening doors that were tightly shut.

Too late I realized... I've flitted my life away
Hear what I tell you and know what I say.

SO ADROIT

My positive thinking just wasn't enough
You invested me with your negative stuff
My life is in this horrible mess
It's because of you, I sadly confess

As I look back to our first night
My arms were open to hold you tight
Your kisses seemed so very right
As I look back to that same night

My heart has exploded, it's shattered to bits
My soul, I know, you can never fix
I fear you'd be up to your old scummy tricks

If I gave you my heart, in need of repair
I know very well you'd never play fair

Wrongly or rightly I have greatly to admit
When my mind goes back, it could have a fit
Because the love you gave was a minute little bit

You took my love, only to exploit
With moves so smooth and so adroit
Yet at the time, it all seemed right
Willingly I gave, without a fight

You boggled my mind to get into my heart
I should have recognized that from the start
It's too late now, I can't go back
The next best thing was to make a new track
It wasn't easy, till I made the start
The healthiest part was from the heart

THE CHOICE

Life is quite extraordinary after all
Just making a decision can be the cure-all
Surrounding myself with an invisible wall,
Profusely persuading that I have it all

When I examined my family roots
I discovered some astounding truths;
Life calls for drastic measures,
I must review what I think are treasures

One can't have all and not be a slave
To material thoughts right to your grave
A decision was made that had to be done
In discarding my possessions, one by one

It's really quite easy when words are voiced
After all, it is only an emotional hoist...

I decided in life I'd let it all happen
I put my thinking cap on and wove a great pattern

I pondered,
I wondered,

I was betwixt and between
There were many things yet that couldn't be seen

I sat for a while
Like being on trial

Having found my common sense,
I blew away that invisible fence

I turned my life to a twist
When I folded my list

MOTHER I LOVE YOU

Often when I say your name
My throat swells up and fills with pain
I know I'll lose you one day
It's a kind of sin I'll have to pay

I love it when you answer to Mum
I adore it when you are my chum
You are there to encourage, you see
You banish the fears that live in me

You often have the presence of mind
That makes you oh, so very kind
You are the finest friend I ever had
You comfort me when I am sad

You are there to share my joys
I can even talk to you of boys
No one will take your place, dear mother
I know I'll never get another

That's what life is all about
My love for you I must shout
Because you are oh, so fine,
I promised the Lord I wouldn't whine
If He'd let you live a real long time

HE KNOWS MY TRAIT

Can't he see I'm only a wench
This burning desire I need him to quench
I may not be responsible for my actions
In this coming event I can't stand the attractions
Give me a sign of some description
From me there will be no objection

I'm talking to him because he is influential
Please think that I have another potential
To the bad I seem to be magnetic
My habits cause me to be energetic

He has the power to change at will
The life I live in this dunghill

He never has to concentrate
So I won't have to hardly wait

He is the only one that knows my trait
Living with it I truly hate

THE PEARL

The Gem is the fruit of a Mollusca shellfish
Gathering one can be a great wish
She's in her abode, you don't have to sieve
Gorgeous to look at, and wonderful to give

It can't be classed as a stone
In spite of that, it's heavenly worn
Doesn't require cutting or polishing
    before its beauty is revealed
What you see is what you get,
    nothing is concealed

She is the aristocrat of the sea,
    and the nobility of the oceans
When we wear the pearl,
    things happen to our emotions

The pearl oyster belongs to the mussel progeny
Whatever it's origin, it costs quite a penny
Pearls can be found that are more than just nice
There are pearls in the world that are beyond price

Wouldn't us girls
Like to fish out those pearls?
The natural state is the best by far
No matter how fussy we really are
If the edges are irregular, that's just right

TOO LATE TO TELL HER

A loved one gone forever more
A loved one lost behind the door
I lost my chance and it's too late
I had many things I wanted to state

We shared very little, there seemed no time
Now looking back, the time was prime
You know how it goes from day to day
I kept putting things off that I wanted to say

When I was born and could not cry
She slapped me hard so I'd not die
She loved me when I lost my teeth
She tried to keep shoes on my feet

I wish that I could fill her shoes
A lot of her traits I would choose

She often went hungry to feed me some
It's hard to conceive that her life is done
She lived her life but had no fun
She toiled and cleaned and did her best
I won't go on, you know the rest

The person I speak of was more than a friend
I loved her dearly right to the end

A LOVING FRIEND

I will never forget you, my wonderful friend
I will treasure my memories right to the end
I think of the times you had to spend
And the broken heart you tried to mend

My life was which way what way, and in a mess
Your carefully chosen words when I was in distress
Oh yes, I feel privileged and grateful, too
To have a dear, dear friend like you

I am enthralled to say you mean the world to me
No, it hasn't taken all this time to see
Did we have an argument or even a pout?
Words got buried, I know, and never ever came out

How could I forget, through all the years
Remember you caused some happy tears
You banished away all my fears
And turned them around to make my cheers
I know you will never be repaid
For the sacrifices you have made
So many, my friend, you've lost count
I can recall them all and shout them out

Everyone flocks to your door
Not because they are hungry or poor
When you greet us with a smile
You really make our lives worthwhile

Your invitations are really precious
Everyone says "Oh! Goodness gracious!"
When you entertain it's always humorous
Your gifts of love are so numerous

I treasure each glorious memory you have given, you see
I know that it will never end, you are inestimable to me
You are always there for one and all
Always at our beck and call
We do appreciate it, especially me
Which I'm sure you can see
Think of the pride I have in you
Others I know agree it's true

In the caring
And the sharing,
Yes, it's true we love you,
But don't you love us too?

I'll never forget you now that we're apart
I'll never forget you, you live in my heart

THE FATHER

Dad always stood out in a crowd
I loved him dearly and I was proud
I would not be here, if it were not for God
I know He rules with a mighty rod

He made some of us strong and others weak
He created in us another cheek
Some of us stand straight and tall
Others feeble and apt to fall

God created us one and all
I'll give Him credit, but that is all
Would I be here, if not for Dad?
You know I wouldn't and that's real sad

I had to wait till he was gone
To realize what he'd passed on
It's too late now to tell him so
And to thank him dearly for what I know

STILL TOMORROW

No matter where you roam
I'll always think you're coming home

You know your voice I'll always hear
Because it gives me a little cheer

Our future is gone, you have left a shadow
It really surprised me, you were not shallow

In spite of the loneliness and the great sorrow
I go on thinking there's still a tomorrow

Out there in the world wherever you be
I hope and I pray you'll return to me

OH WHY OH WHY

I wonder why he fled
Especially now, ready to wed
He's the one that wouldn't wait
He was so adamant about the date
I've known him only a month or two
Maybe that was much too few

I do not wish to boast
His sexy kiss I'll miss the most
Of course, he was the perfect host
When we talked of child and wife
He hid nothing and talked of life
He told me he had done his thing
I assured I'd had my fling
I just can't imagine why
He left me high and dry

I am only seventy four
This man of sixty I adore
We discussed the things that we should share
We even talked of what to wear
Difficult topics like our death bed
Sincerely were the things he said

When he saw that I wore a wig
He said he didn't care a fig
I wonder why, oh, why
He has left me high and dry

I thought that he would surely cry
When on the nightstand he saw my eye
It didn't even make him blink
That really put him in the pink
I really wonder why, oh, why
He just left me high and dry

When I spoke to him of my one deaf ear,
Words of love he said I'd hear
I love him dearly even to this day
Why did he leave me and go away

I felt for sure he'd lay an egg
When he detected my wooden leg
His being so good and kind
He assured me he didn't mind
I still wonder why, oh, why
He just left me high and dry . . .

We had the rehearsal, it went quite well
He asked many questions but I won't tell
He signed all the papers I had asked him to
He even said loudly "I love you"
He signed them all with a grin
I felt right then I had the win

At the end when he read all
He straightened up and looked quite tall
He wasn't the same, he seemed very ill
Do you think he thought they were my will?

He bade me farewell and said goodbye
I really wonder why, oh, why
He just left me high and dry

Could it be the prenuptial he had signed
That made him change his mind?
My ex-husband that was the lawyer
Had put my papers in perfect order

MY LOVE

I love you more than words can say
And it grows deeper day by day
In every thought and every way
More than words can ever say.

You mean the earth and stars to me
The most wonderful person I ever did see
And I do want our love to be
Even better for you than it is for me.

I want to spend my life with you
Share everything I think and do
Because these words are oh, so true
My darling, my love, I DO LOVE YOU !!!

STOLEN LOVE

I'm supposed to be happy because I'm so in love
But I know I need guidance from the One up above
Loving you darling is not to be abused
My mind is a turmoil and very confused

The nights are long and I can not sleep
Into my mind you always creep
I miss you very much it seems
If I close my eyes, you enter my dreams

I can see the contours of your face
I can feel your hugs and your firm embrace
Knowing you, darling, has left it's trace
And now you're off wondering somewhere in space

Your many kisses I can not erase
And I want to feel your handsome face
I can still remember your gentle touch
Oh darling, I love you very much

I'm supposed to be happy because I'm so in love
Yet I wait for an answer from Him above
I know you're many miles away
Often I sit and pray and pray
Why don't You just show me the way?

Like the darkest clouds up in the sky
They need not be there, please tell me why
You are the Almighty, You can answer me
But... are You listening to my plea?

I'm supposed to be happy because I'm so in love
Give me the reasons why You stole my love

GODGIVEN

Thank you, Lord, for such a friend
We know they're all Yours to give or to lend
I had her for years, that's quite true
And I would't have found her if it were not for You

We shared a great lot from the time that we met
We laughed and we cried, though her moods were set
I'd known her forever in my little mind
And thanked You fondly for my great find

I know You thought the time was right
You came and took her in the dark of night
I didn't find her till the very next day
Oh, there was so much I wanted to say

I'd say it now, if only I could,
Her quality of life was not very good
I'd change it all now, believe me, I would

Many sad people she left behind
She was the sort that was very kind
There were many things she did so well
I should have told her that she was swell.
It's too late now, I lost my chance
To tell her the things she did enhance.

The person I speak of was more than a friend
She was the lady that bore me that I loved to the end.

SECOND CHANCE

Our lives gallop by so fast
Don't revert to the past
Just give me a chance
At a little romance

I will plant a seed
No, not a weed
When it grows
It need not be a rose
But let's see what it shows

I could put you in a heavenly trance
Your mind and soul I will enhance
If you'll only give me a second chance
At a little romance

A LONG TIME COMING

It wasn't easy when I chose
To end a marriage that had froze
There was no one to share with me
Or help me so I could feel free

It was hard for me to strive
For that quality and drive
And hope to find a friend
Who would coax me to the end

It took a while for me to find
That life nor I wasn't blind
I looked for that special kind
Which was very, very hard to find

Then one day you did appear
I felt with you there was no fear
Soon you were in my heart
Then I felt we'd never part

Life's pathways often bend
We are lucky if we reach the end
However, you're my pal and friend
Please love me to the end

I WONDER WHY

I think of all the splendid things I want,
    none of which I need
It never does occur to me
    that all of it is greed
I'm living for so many things
    to happen just for me
I never think of unfortunate ones,
    imprisoned, who ought be free

I'll tightly clutch a bag of things
    that I have newly bought
I'll pass a vagrant on the street
    and refuse to give a thought
I hoard and store all the things
    that I have ever sought
I very seldom give away,
    although I know I ought

I hardly ever get some mail
    and rarely on the phone
I wonder why I have no friends,
    I'm always on my own
Someone had the gall to go
    and ask me for some bucks
I need not tell you what I gave,
    his reply was that "it sucks"

I wonder why I'm all alone
    and crippled in this bed
I wonder why they passed me by
    and left me nearly dead

YOU ARE MY EVERYTHING

Darling, you are my everything,
    you're my dream come true
No matter what should happen,
    I'll always think of you
You taught me to think a different way,
    with many things to seek
Because you are so special,
    and in many ways unique

I had the world at my feet,
    yet it's you that I adore
You turned a knob inside me
    and opened up a door
I thought I'd travel far and wide
    to visit many a shore
The thought of leaving you behind,
    cured me forever more

MY DEAREST

I think of you
   in a very exceptional way
And the love I have for you,
   my dearest, is in a special way
I now can see the entrance
   to a future bright and clear
You have opened up my narrow mind,
   and thrown away my fear

When you gave to me
   that round, gold band
You took my happiness
   in the palm of your hand
My love for you,
   I know you won't abuse,
And bad of you,
   I hope I'll never accuse

My heartfelt love is very strong
I know this love can't be wrong
I have put you on a pedestal
And I intend to serve you well

EDICTS

Laugh
Cry
Experiment

Organize
Think big
Step through the sieve

Plan
With innovations
And explorations
Throughout your life

MY DARLING I LOVE YOU

How many ways do I love you . . .
Start counting the drops of the morning dew
That's how much I love you

How many times do I say your name
To count the shore sand would give you pain
You are as precious to me as a priceless pearl
I've loved you since you were a prosaic girl

I love you from your head to your toes
To me you're like a red, red rose
Even when there is a complaint
To me you're like a pious saint

I love you more than the dew drop on the fragrant flower
That, my dear, is your heavenly power
Being with you is Christmas and holly
Seldom suffering melancholy

I've put you on a pedestal
I did it all with my free will
I'll love you till the waters still

MATERIAL CHANGES

You made me feel I had no scruples
Obsessed by money such as dollars, pounds, and rubles
I talked of only material things,
The car,the house, the family jewels
Living according to my own rules

Without saying a word you penetrate
You banished in me all the hate
When we are together, just you and me
There's a tremendous change that I can see
You don't have to say or do a thing
It seems to come from somewhere within

At last I hear your acclamation
Your comment and your demonstration
This attitude of mine required removal
It leaves with your enthusiastic approval

When we met we were miles apart
Now I love you so much and it's right from my heart
I never thought I'd gain your admiration
Always feeling like a poor relation
You didn't have to dictate
You don't have that ugly trait
At last you decided to venerate

You taught me to have morality
And before that it was integrity

BEFORE I MET YOU

Life has become wonderful since we met
Every day is glorious, especially for me
I'll never leave you, that you can bet

I have grown since I met you
Inside and out, it shines right through
You know what, it's all due to you

I'd like to think I did my part, too
In loving and sharing and holding you
I hope that I taught you a few things, too
Like being honest and caring your whole life through

Life would be wonderful if you will enhance
All the good things, and expect a fair chance
Accept the best, keep lighthearted, give of yourself,
And that will be rewarding just in itself
Be kind and considerate, have no pretense
And most of all - hold no suspense

It was a mere existence, day by day
Till you came along and changed my way
I now wonder how I lived before I met you
Because all that I am is due to you

HUGS AND KISSES

I am going to invest in kisses and hugs
A far better cure than the potency of drugs
Like flickering candles in the dark
A hug and a kiss will leave their mark.

OWED TO HIM

Suddenly I saw a familiar face
I walked faster to pick up the pace
To my surprise it was my friend
When I last saw him, he was at his end

His last requests were little ones
He told me where to find the funds
Hard to speak but he uttered some
He praised me a lot and called me 'chum'

He gave instructions with each request
His lovely girl he spoke of best
He couldn't extend a hand to me
Not because it wasn't free

I'll remember this to my dying day
There were certain things I wanted to say
When I last saw him, he was a shell
My name, my face, he couldn't tell

His eyes were open yet he was blind,
To the multitude of sins I had to hide
Never letting him know I married his bride,
Stole his savings and swept him aside

In my mind, he was surely dead
Suddenly my conscience I fiercely dread
I patted his shoulder and bid him farewell
Cause this hero's story I can never tell

DON'T LET IT GET YOU DOWN

Just because you are sick or sore
Doesn't mean you leave the shore

Even if the courage you get is somewhat raw
Invite it in and begin to draw
You have the power within yourself
Start to practice to leave the shelf

Sick or sore
Find the cure
Skinny or fat
You can fix that

If you have AIDS there is no answer
A lot more hope if you have cancer
There's such a thing as making a mistake
If it were only so, for your sad sake
The principle thing is to know where you're at
Discover that!

You're on the right track
Go ahead and unpack
Don't ever get that far down
Threatening your future to leave your hometown
DON'T LET IT GET YOU DOWN

NOTHING IS MULTIFARIOUS ANYMORE

Some things can't be hurried,
   one of them is wine
I want to do so many things,
   but I never have the time
I remember as a child
   when times were oh, so great
Dinner was never ready,
   we always had to wait
We are now so sophisticated,
   we just pop in a pack
Supermarkets are full of them,
   we buy them by the stack

When you've made all the purchases
   and you're standing at the till
The girl is automatic,
   nothing is at will
You don't need multiplication,
   to count is like a sin,
You pull out a plastic object
   and you pay up with a grin

When I look for things for my repast
What's most important is it cooks real fast
There is no such thing as grilled or boiled
Cause the food is in a tin or foiled
I never think of extravagance, or being a gourmet
I just think of the time I have,
   not what I have to pay
It seems nothing much is multifarious any more
In fact there's nothing left that I adore

ENVY

I happen to love the style myself
Coming from me that won't help
I like it 'cause it's sad and gritty
With merging lines disgustingly witty

Analyzing the material prose,
He plants the seed that grows and grows
It's often majestic, noble and royal
Fantastically great, that's his style

Feeling very inordinate
Some thin line is moderate

Don't stop now, you mustn't quit
Others are the opposite
When he's full of his esteem
He can go to great extreme

His language gets a little rough
He's showing off and being tough
When you think he's left you in the lurch
Don't believe it, he's off to church

Turning a head and snubbing a nose
Some great men read his prose
Later when they thought to mock it
They produced it from their pocket

Just when you think 'he's not human'
That's when he's got you almost droolin'
Some people thought that he wrote trash
Can you do better, have a bash!
Cause that's the stuff that brought in the cash
And made famous Ogden Nash

If I was asked to pen an inscription
"A sensation!" would be my description

AN ANSWER

A while ago I made a request
He said no, but I didn't accept.
I waited a while and I asked again,
He didn't refuse, but He didn't give in.
When I look back now, I do understand
He only had my best interest in hand.

You see, I didn't wait the appointed time,
I thought I knew more than our Divine.
I took on a task that I'm still in
The anguish and worries are penance for my sin.

So once again, I make a request
Dear Lord, please get me out of this mess.
I'll never, ever, play God again
No matter what state I'm in.

REJOICE

For those who are left behind,
Not knowing what they will find.

Rejoice! I am no longer afraid
Yet I don't know if I have prayed,
Or if confessions have been made
For my soul to save.
Or if my body meets the grave.

I may not have been ready when He came,
But He took me just the same.
He gives no medals or fancy tags
Nor does He care if we wear rags.

He doesn't ignore my enemy, to Him it's another soul
When He hears the moan of a solder hiding in a hole.
We seemed to one another like devils found on earth
But what really matters is: in heaven, He knows our worth.
Enemies in battle, but together at heaven's gate
Each soul judged on goodness, weighed on every trait.

Please don't worry about me,
At last, I am set free.
Rejoice, take comfort from one another,
Knowing I am home, one way or the other.

MY OLD LOVER

Someone used to be my lover
Sure, I've replaced him with another
I've found myself a predictable one
And we'll be sure to have some fun

This time I know I've found the best
He has even passed the cruelest test
So time with him I will invest

I thought I was only on an intermission
Till suddenly I didn't need permission,
To laugh and cry and be myself
Emotionally I didn't need your help

He has caused in me a great sensation
While I have for him great admiration
He portrays outstanding concern for me
And when we're wed we'll soon be three

I was extremely lucky to ever find
This dear man that's one of a kind
This is the one that I adore
Day by day I love him more

My love for him has no apprehension
He gives me all the right attention
I wonder if you had not changed place
Would you ever have had his gentle grace

TAKE THIS ADVICE

A tragedy happened a few years ago
And looking back, there wasn't much show
It wasn't that good and not much fun
I could see right then what I should have done

My troubles then put me in a spin
Only just then did my life begin
I started to live in spite of the facts
And started right in to cover my tracks

I became the good person that I should have been
And uncovered the real ugliness and the sin
I should not have waited to get such a shock
To discover that I lived my life as a mock

It's never too late to make a new start
In doing so, let it come from the heart
And know that in life we take what is dealt
There's more to life than counting our wealth

Please recognize - this is a fact
Take a lesson from me, don't risk an attack
Don't chance it happening, we can't bring you back

DIET

We're talking about size
Or being pennywise and our waistline's demise
This is for the guys and of course the gals
Or anyone out there that we want for pals

You will have to check your own condition
Remove yourself from all suspicion
It's up to you all, to change if you will
Instead of the pan you'll use the grill

Especially if you want to hear the word 'thin'
Just follow instructions and you will win
You're going to use a lot of willpower
Thinking thin almost every hour

You'll have to do some exercise, too
To look in the mirror at the lovely new you
You'll have great pains down in your gut
Your stomach will think your throat has been cut

It's hours now since you ate a thing
A demanding voice says "eat again"
Another is asking, "why did you begin?"
Your brain is screaming "I'm going to give in!"

Today you decided to throw in the towel
When an old friend encouraged and gave you a howl
He could have been lying, but you don't give a fig
You have defiantly decided you're going to be big.

Yet you've certainly converted and changed a lot
There is very little that cooks in your pot.
Convinced all sweets are part of a plot
Being tempted by one, you ate the whole lot!

To remind you of your final goal,
And the calories that you often stole
Hangs your fat photo of before,
Grinning at you on your fridge door

Needing your appetite to somehow vanish,
As you are absolutely famished
You have a dreadful craving
But your appetite you are saving
No, not for chocolate cake
But for roast beef or steak
While candy or brandy ceased to exist
It is now tonic water served with a twist

You've had the nightmares right through the night
They won't be excuses, you'll keep up the fight
By blacklisting sweets and getting a rose
Already your thoughts are of buying new clothes

It was your primary goal from the spring to the fall
To your great astonishment, you did it all
You go to the closet, not a thing to wear
Gee, you are hilariously happy...
    NOW THAT YOU ARE THERE!

YOU THOUGHT YOU HAD NOTHING TO GIVE

I've heard you've had a great disrupt
Suffering the state of being bankrupt
I know your morale is badly hurt
Especially now that you've lost your shirt

"I have nothing left that I can share"
I have heard you repeat it, deep in prayer
This you have, and can surely give
By giving again you'll begin to live

There's something you forgot to do today
The golden rule is to give away
You have nothing left, that's what you say
There's always something to give away
It might be hiding, but I know it's there
You've nearly forgotten how to share

You'll always know where it went
It will cost you nothing, not even a cent
You'll be given a precious and prompt receipt,
From the one that receives it, it will be a treat

You say you've had nothing to give in a while
I say you have, and it's always in style
When you were doing well you always passed it
It's easy to remember, it was your biggest asset
Now you remember, it is your heavenly smile
That you haven't used in a great, great while

A grin or smile, it's yours to give
If it turns to laughter, you'll start to live
Give it a go with all your might
In doing so, you'll see the light
There's nothing wrong, you just lost your fight
And isn't it a blessing it wasn't your sight

There's no great sin in being poor
You'll pick up again, of that I'm sure
Smile, get fruitful, and don't be curt
It's a transitional time and you're not really hurt

A TOAST

I drink to your health
I pray for your wealth
Did I hear a shout
That I left something out

What can that be?
You want all three!
With a great big yell,
Happiness you tell

I'll put some in there
Just to be fair
I'm glad that you care
It's nice to share
For that you must pay
That does not come free
Not even from me

Health, wealth and happiness ... you see!
Now that you've been given all three,
You should be full of joy and glee.

CHANGES

There comes a time to say goodbye
Even though you cry and cry

It's now the time to step aside
You don't need me by your side
Life is what you make of it
It's time you went and did your bit

Life to you is in a daze
You travel through it like a maze
You know that you can clear the haze
Start spending your life so that it pays

You can't see a living thing
In fact to you, your life is grim
Sure, you know what you have to do
That big, big world awaits for you

It's time for you to say goodbye
There's no time left for you to cry
Try to give yourself away
You'll be surprised how it will pay

A CANDIDATE

They don't make 'em any more,
That's for sure
At least not as precious as you.
The ingredients are the best by far,
When they were creating you.

I really feel proud when you're around,
Even when we are alone.
I want to share you, that's true,
I'm fussy with who!
They have to be sincere and true.

You're gentle and kind, it's an angel I've found
Angelic in every way.
You're thoughtful and good with a heart of gold
In fact you are a treasure to me.

The beautiful thing is, you've rubbed off on me
And people can see the change.
It's not very much but I hope it's enough
For a candidate to be saved.

NO OTHER CHANCE

I started crying
When I heard you were dying
Could it be you took some, too?
Making me responsible for you

A voice that came from deep within
Told me then I harbored a sin
I'm praying now, my soul is rent
You're close to going, your life is spent

I am not ashamed to admit I was wrong
I'm terribly weak, I've never been strong
You didn't complain, you let me sin
You knew in the end you would win

You decided to evaporate
The pressure of living you found too great

I never gave you sweet perfume
I never ever played you a tune
I never gave you much in life
Suddenly thinking of the afterlife

GONE AWAY

I have memories that I can hold
You have nothing, you were bold
You have gone away without saying goodbye
I can't forgive you, though I try
You left me behind like an old, old toy
Robbed of feelings, robbed of joy

I recognize now
When we took the vow
To tell the truth, you didn't know how
Telling me you loved me didn't mean a thing
You even told me it would never wear thin
You treated our love just like a game
Somehow you seem to have no shame

I have memories embedded in me
From the past there are things I can see
I realize now you needed me
I gave you my wisdom, I set you free

I have memories that I still hold
They'll stay with me till I am cold
Many times you tried to make me sin
Wasn't I glad I never gave in
When I look back now it's with a grin

I gave you wisdom, that's true
But without me, it won't work for you
I bet you're thinking that I am mad
While sitting at home and feeling sad
You couldn't be more wrong, my pal
I ran right out and got me a gal
The love we share we equally divide
We both feel a great sense of pride
It's more wonderful knowing we have nothing to hide

I have memories of you I'll take to my grave
They have taught me the lesson that I used to crave
That in life it's important to give and take
And find a partner that's not a fake

HARD TO FATHOM

Your love is a spasmodic, challenging affair
Your emotions are forever changing,
Though you are not aware

Your allusions are as deep as the ocean
With the surge of an incoming tide
It washes ashore a love to adore
And sometimes I'm sure I'll abide

Your attention, your love and affection
Have returned again to the sea,
I can sense the change in your direction,
But not altogether leaving me

Your heart is a wonder, ever at sea
Somewhere in your heart, there's a place for me

I know that you are searching your dream, on a new shore
You've mounted the curliest wave
You and your imagination are off once more

POIGNANT PAIN

No reason was given
So my tears are well hidden
I am left with a token
A heart that's all broken

I still have memories, too
Were you too good to be true?
I wonder did I have a tutor
Who made me wiser for the future?

Yet beneath this poignant pain
I can feel a sense of gain
Although our love could not be stronger
It could have gone on much, much longer

I felt nothing wrong
Our friendship was so strong
My love and affection, I freely gave
Being with you, I felt so brave

I must not have a pang of fear
Let the past be gone, my future's here

PROSPEROUS PLOT

Are you viewing life from a foreign shore?
You should be thinking as an entrepreneur
You can open the door to great wealth
And still retain the picture of health

You don't have to take hard knocks
In your head there are no rocks
Think of the trees when they blossom
Tiny buds, yet they look awesome

Even if your life is in a terrible mess
Don't think of failure, think of success
Please try this and I guarantee
You'll find life great, just like me

We have to believe in ourselves
Or we could end up on the shelves
God gives us ideas, to use our brain
In doing so we gain our fame

We ought to find out if we are entrepreneurs
To think and to say and become great doers
We can choose to do or not
But we should give it our best shot
Invent for yourself a prosperous plot

Don't look for the impossible that you know you won't get
It will make you frustrated, and start you to fret
When you feel down because of rejection
Look in the mirror for a good reflection
Fortify yourself with a big smile
You will journey right back to run that last mile

You will have done your bit, there will be a lot to show
You will be ready to meet Him when you go
In using all your imagination
It will have gotten you to your destination

Around yourself you had built a wall
Being protective, in case you would fall
You had it all, it was there within
You just didn't know where or how to begin
And looking back you can say with a grin
You knew all the time that you would win

ONLY TODAY

Never look back
To cover a track
Just enjoy today

You can't make a borrow
Or pay for tomorrow
Or any other day

The thing to remember
And not to hinder
The quality we have today

Don't worry about tomorrow
Or any great sorrow
Just enjoy today!